Mom Hacks

40 Genius Tricks to Make Kids CRAVE Healthy Food & Quit Junk (Without Fights!)

If you're tired of your child's tantrums, picky eating, junk cravings, and mealtime battles... this book will feel like a miracle. These 40 genius hacks are real, practical, tested on my own child, and used by 1,000+ moms in my community."

How I Stopped My Kid from Begging for Junk & Made Him Eat Healthier Food—Without Fights or Bribing!

by Meenakshi Rana

KAVYA
PUBLICATIONS

Publisher:

SDR INNOWAYS INDIA PVT. LTD.
667, Rajaward, Kulpahar, Mahoba - 210426

Imprint:
KAVYA PUBLICATIONS
Plot No.107C, Hanuman Khand, Gulabvatika, Behta Hazipur, Loni-UP (Near Dilshad Garden Delhi) NCR -201102

Mob.	: 7905266820
Website	: www.kavyapublications.com
E-Mail	: info@kavyapublications.com

ISBN	: 978-93-6431-095-6
Price	: 299/-INR
Year	: 2025

This book is printed at MTL and published by author Ajay Agrawal, CEO of SDR Innoways India Pvt. Ltd. Kulpahar Mahoba with its imprint and centre, Kavya Publications Delhi.

Disclaimer

This book is a work of nonfiction based on the author's personal experiences and knowledge. While every effort has been made to ensure the accuracy of the information herein, this book is not intended as medical advice. It is not intended to diagnose, treat, cure, or prevent any disease, nor to substitute professional medical advice. Readers should consult qualified professionals regarding their specific circumstances. Neither the publisher nor the author shall be liable for any loss of profit or health or any other commercial damages, including but not limited to special, incidental, consequential or other damages.

Cover design and illustrations by Meenakshi Rana
Editing by Meenakshi Rana

For more resources, visit:
Instagram: Fitfamilyhitfamily
YouTube: Fitfamilyhitfamily

Dedication

To my son, **Khushhal Rana**,
My love for him and his health inspired every hack of this book.

And to my biggest Cheer leader my husband,
Dharmender Rana,
whose constant encouragement and belief in me gave me the courage to share my knowledge with the world.

To every **Mom** who wants to raise strong, happy, healthy kids—without the stress.

To our vibrant community, **FitFamilyHitFamily**,
on a mission to make **one million families healthier**—one habit at a time.

Table of Contents

Bonus Chapter

Introduction: The Secret to Raising a Healthy Eater

Do you feel frustrated every time your child refuses vegetables but happily munches on chips and candy? Are you tired of bribing, begging, or battling at mealtimes?

I've been there. And I discovered: **you don't need to fight to make your kids eat better—you just need to outsmart their cravings.**

I'm a nutritionist but I'm a mom too who learned to "hack" my kid's psychology and taste buds. What started as trial and error turned into 40 powerful strategies that helped me raise a healthy eater—without shouting, bribes, or guilt trips.

In this book, you'll find everything I've learned, including:

- Why your child really craves junk (hint: it's not just taste)
- How to make veggies and fruits more desirable than chips
- How to reduce sugar cravings without making your kid feel "punished"
- How to rewire their taste buds—without them even noticing!

This isn't about restriction. It's about **replacing**, **reinventing**, and **rewiring**. And yes, your child can still enjoy a treat or two—without going overboard.

Chapter 1:

Why Kids Love Junk Food (And How to Change It!)

"Mom, I Want Chips!" – Understanding Your Child's Cravings

Have you ever noticed how kids light up when they see a packet of chips or a chocolate bar but turn up their noses at vegetables? You're not alone! If you've ever wondered why kids seem addicted to junk food, the answer lies in **science**, **psychology**, and **smart marketing**.

In this chapter, we'll uncover:

☑ **Why kids naturally crave sugar and junk food**
☑ **How food companies secretly manipulate our children's taste buds**
☑ **The hidden ingredients that keep them coming back for more**
☑ **Mom's Secret Strategy: The 3-Step Junk Detox (Without Fights!)**

🔍 The Science Behind Junk Food Addiction

Our children aren't born craving fries, cookies, or soda—it's something they learn over time. Here's why junk food becomes so irresistible to them:

1️⃣ **The Sugar Trap:** Junk food is loaded with **sugar**, which triggers the brain to release **dopamine**, the "feel-good" chemical. The more sugar kids eat, the more they crave it—just like a cycle of addiction.

2️⃣ **The Fat-Salt-Sugar Combo:** Most packaged snacks are a perfect mix of **fat, salt, and sugar**, making them *hyper-palatable* (which means our brains want more and more!).

3️⃣ **Marketing Tricks on Kids:** Have you noticed how junk food brands use **bright colors**, **fun mascots**, and **catchy jingles**? Companies spend billions targeting kids so that they associate **happiness** with their products.

4️⃣ **Hidden Additives & Flavors:** Many processed foods contain **artificial flavor enhancers** like MSG, which make kids feel like regular food is too bland. This is why a child who eats flavored chips often rejects plain, home-cooked meals.

🚨 The Hidden Danger: How Junk Food Affects Your Child's Health

---

We often think a little bit of junk is okay, but the real danger is in how it **rewires their eating habits**. Here's what happens:

⚠ **Weakened Immunity** – Kids eating too much sugar & processed food get sick more often.
⚠ **Mood Swings & Tantrums** – Sugar crashes lead to crankiness & emotional meltdowns.
⚠ **Low Energy & Focus** – Junk food doesn't provide real energy, making kids sluggish.
⚠ **Taste Bud Damage** – Over time, kids stop liking natural foods like fruits & veggies.

The good news? You **CAN reset your child's cravings** with a simple strategy!

✨ Mom's Secret - 3 Hacks Junk Detox (No Tantrums!)

If you try to forcefully ban junk food, it often backfires (because kids want what they can't have!). Instead, follow this **3-step detox** to gradually shift their habits—**without fights or stress.**

Mom Hacks

Hack 1#: The "Invisible Swap" Trick

Instead of suddenly removing junk food, start **replacing it** with healthier, tastier alternatives:

🍿 *Instead of Chips* → Popcorn with Butter & Herbs
🍫 *Instead of Chocolate Bars* → Dark Chocolate Almond Clusters
🥤 *Instead of Sugary Juice* → Fruit-Infused Water with Mint

Mom Action Plan:

✔Make these swaps **gradually**, so your child doesn't feel like they're "missing out."

Hack 2#: The "Supermarket Power Play"

❌ **DON'T** buy junk food at home – Kids can't crave what's not there!
☑️ **DO** let them choose between healthy snacks – "Do you want a banana smoothie or apple slices with peanut butter?"
🧑‍🍳 **DO** involve them in cooking – Kids love food they help prepare!

Hack 3#: The "Fun Food Challenge" Game

Kids love games, challenges, and rewards! Here's how to turn healthy eating into a **fun weekly challenge**:

🎉 The "**Rainbow Plate**" Challenge – Eat 5 different colored foods a day to earn a sticker.

THE 'RAINBOW PLATE' CHALLENGE
Eat 5 different coloured foods a day to earn a sticker

🎉 The "**Taste Test" Game** – Blindfold them & let them guess healthy foods.

🎉 The "**No Sugar Day" Reward** – A fun surprise if they avoid sugar for 24 hours.

By gamifying healthy eating, kids get **excited about it instead of resisting!**

Hack #4: Understand the Real Enemy - Dopamine🧠

Why kids get addicted to junk?

Junk food isn't just tasty—it's designed to hijack your child's brain. Every sugary bite or crunchy chip gives them a quick dopamine hit (the "feel-good" hormone). Over time, their brain starts associating joy with junk.

The Problem: Healthy food like 🥦 Broccoli doesn't give that same instant "high." So, naturally, your child wants more chips, less spinach.

The Hack: Use "dopamine triggers" in a smarter way.

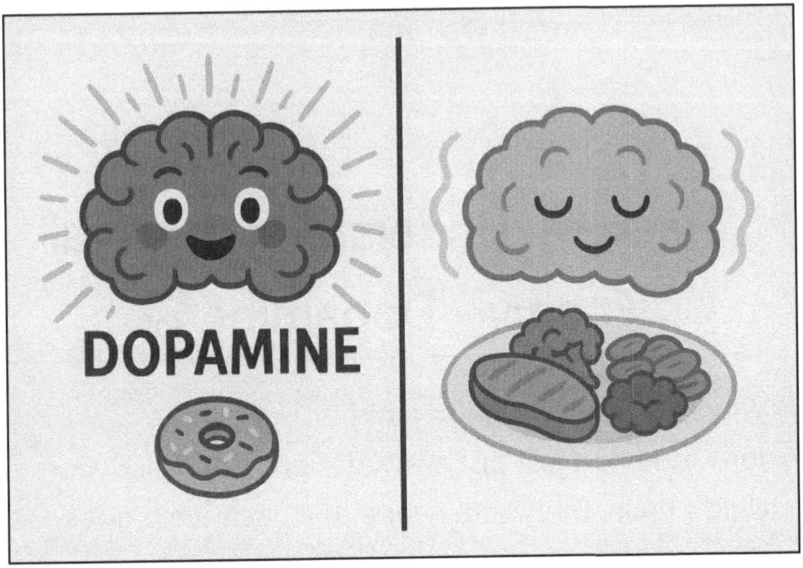

Mom Action Plan 👩‍👧:

☑ **Pair healthy food with praise**: Add a high-five, a cheer, or a sticker when they eat veggies.
☑ **Create fun food stories**: "Superman loves spinach!" Make it playful.
☑ **Slowly reduce sugar hits**: Cut junk gradually so their taste buds reset and real food starts tasting better.

Takeaway: Your Child CAN Love Healthy Food!

Kids aren't naturally addicted to junk food—it's something they learn. But just like **bad habits are learned, good habits can be taught too!** By using **psychology**, **smart swaps**, and **fun challenges**, you can **retrain your child's cravings** and make them **love healthy food without fights or bribing.**

Chapter 2:

The "No More Junk" Strategy – Making Unhealthy Food Boring

WHAT THEY CAN'T SEE...
CHIPS
THEY WON'T CRAVE!

🍟 How I Made My Child Lose Interest in Junk Food

You know what's harder than saying no to your child's puppy eyes asking for pizza or chips? Saying it again tomorrow. And the day after.

[Speech Bubble Illustration: Child saying "Can I please have just ONE more chip?" and mom replying "Sure... but you'll get the same tomorrow too!"]

I realized: instead of **fighting** junk food, what if I made it... **boring**?

🚫 Why "Banning" Junk Doesn't Work

They love it because it's **exciting, restricted, and rewarded**.

So I **flipped the script**.

I **stopped making junk food the enemy**... I made it **uninteresting**

😘 Hack #5: The 3-Step Junk Food Detox (Without Tantrums)

Step 1: "It's Always There" – Kill the Excitement

A jar of untouched cookies with cobwebs forming

"It's there... but no one cares!"

It's there...
but no one cares!

HACK #33: BUILDING THE "TASTEBUD RESET MENU"

Changing the plate without the fight

Week 2 was all about cleaning up meals—but **secretly**.
I replaced ketchup with homemade tomato dip, fried chips with roasted makhana, and hid veggie purée inside parathas.
He didn't notice.
He just said, *"Why is today's food so yummy?"*

Mom's Action Plan:

✔ Swap 1 unhealthy item per day with a cleaner option 🔁

✔ Use hidden veggies & tasty sauces 🥕 🧄

✔ Don't announce changes—let their taste buds adjust silently 🤫

✔ Create your own "New Family Favorites" list 📝

HACK #34: THE "SECRET REWARD SYSTEM"

Motivation without bribery

Every time my son hit ⭐ ⭐ ⭐ ⭐ ⭐ on his meal chart, he unlocked a **non-food reward**—a new storybook 📚, a movie night 🎬, or 30 extra minutes of playtime ⏱️. Soon, he started asking, *"What's my mission today, Mom?"*

Mom's Action Plan:

✔ Use a reward system that celebrates **consistency**, not perfection 🌟

✔ Avoid food as a bribe—choose **creative treats** 🎨

✔ Let kids **design their own rewards list** 🧒 📝

✔ Track visually—charts, stickers, or even a **superhero wall** 🦸

HACK #35: CELEBRATE THE 30-DAY HERO TRANSFORMATION

Turn the journey into a celebration

At the end of 30 days, we threw a **Healthy Hero Party** at home.
There was a fruit bar 🍓, superhero wraps 🦸, and he proudly received his **"Smart Eater" certificate**.
There was no cake—and he didn't miss it.
He just said, *"Can I make that banana smoothie again tomorrow?"*

Mom's Action Plan:

- ✔ Plan a **Healthy Party** as a celebration—not a reward 🎉
- ✔ Involve your child in **cooking and decorating** 🧁
- ✔ Award a **certificate or medal**—make them feel proud 🏅
- ✔ Keep momentum with a **"Next 30 Days" tracker** 📅

CHAPTER WRAP-UP:

In just 30 days, you've:

- Swapped tantrums for teamwork
- Replaced junk with joy
- Turned your kitchen into a superhero lab

And you didn't just change what your child eats...
You **transformed how they think about food.**

Healthy Kid
Happy Mom

HACK #36: Grocery Shopping with Kids—Turn It into a Fun Adventure 🛒🍎

Instead of dreaded shopping trips, I made it a game. We created a list with pictures and assigned my son a "Mission" to find all the healthy items. He loved being my "helper," and it made the trip feel exciting!

Mom's Action Plan:

- ✔ Create a visual list with fun symbols 🖼
- ✔ Give your child "mission tasks" at the store 🔍
- ✔ Celebrate their success with a high-five or sticker 🌟

HACK #37: The "Snack Drawer" Trick -Organizing Healthy Choices 🍪🥕

Instead of letting the pantry overwhelm us with junk, I set up a snack drawer with only healthy options. Now, when my son is hungry, he can pick from the drawer without needing my approval.

Mom's Action Plan:

✔ Pre-pack healthy snacks into easy-to-reach containers 🍊

✔ Label them with fun names—"Power Bites" or "Superfruit Packs" 🍇

✔ Keep the treats hidden for special occasions 🎉

CHAPTER 10

WHEN LOVE COMES WITH LADDOOS

How to Handle Guests, Grandparents & Relatives—Without Losing Your Mind (or Your Meal Plan)

Sometimes it's not your child—but the *well-meaning guests and loving relatives* who throw off your healthy eating rhythm.
One visit, one wedding, one vacation… and suddenly your child's sugar detox is out the window!

Here's how to **honor their love** while still protecting your child's habits—*without drama, guilt, or food fights.*

Because sometimes love comes wrapped in a box of sweets… and you need a smart, kind plan!
Let's dive in!

🍬❤️👵👨‍👩‍👧‍👦🍽️💪

HACK #38: 👵 Grandparent Pampering—From Sugar Bombs to Smart Snacks 🍬➡️🥜

They mean well, but... it's raining sweets again.
Instead of arguing, I got my mom involved—she now makes **"Nani's Immunity Ladoo"** with jaggery, dates, and dry fruits.
My son thinks they're magic.

Mom's Action Plan:

✔ Create healthy alternatives *with* grandparents together

✔ Name the recipes after them ("Dadi's Power Mix") 👴 👵

✔ Educate gently—show how it helps the child 💖

✔ Turn them into your nutrition allies 🤝

HACK #39: 🎁 Gifts from Guests- Handling Junk with Grace 🍪 🍫

I started a **"Share & Save" box**. My son gets to choose one treat to keep, and we donate the rest.

No guilt. No drama. And the guests don't even notice!

Mom's Action Plan:

- ✔ Talk to your child *before* the guests arrive 🗣
- ✔ Create a "treat limit" rule you both agree on ☑
- ✔ Use a "Thank You, Now Share" basket or box 🎉
- ✔ Later swap the junk for a surprise reward or activity

HACK #40: 🧳 Staying at Nani/Mama House—Vacation Without Food Rebellion 🍭 🥦

Every vacation turned into a junk fest... until I made a "Super Kid Agreement."

We created a chart with 3 rules:

1️⃣ One junk item a day

2️⃣ Add one healthy food at each meal

3️⃣ Call Mom with your Power Plate!

Nani loved being part of the mission.

Mom's Action Plan:

- ✔ Set fun ground rules *before* they leave ✈
- ✔ Make relatives part of the "healthy fun" mission 👵
- ✔ Send healthy snack packs along 🥜
- ✔ Use video calls to cheer on their progress 📱

Bonus Chapter

Eat Hard or Eat Smart: Why Supplements Are Your Secret Weapon for Raising Healthy Kids

Every mom wants her child to eat well, grow tall, stay active, and avoid junk food. But in real life?
School stress, unpredictable hunger, evening cravings, and picky eating make it nearly **impossible** for kids to meet all their nutrition needs through food alone.

This is where **smart supplementation** becomes your best friend.
Not to replace food — but to **fill the gaps** so your child's body feels nourished, stable, and supported.

And when their body is nourished?
You'll be shocked how quickly **junk cravings disappear**.

Let's break it down.

Why Supplements Matter Today (More Than Ever)

Kids today face challenges we never did:

- Nutrient-loss in soil
- Busy school routines
- Increased screen time
- Processed food exposure
- Reduced outdoor play
- Inconsistent appetite

Even if you cook healthy meals, your child may still be **missing key nutrients** that support gut health, brain function, growth, and immunity.

You can't stand in the kitchen all day.
But you *can* give their body what it needs in a smarter way.

3 Essential Supplements Every Growing Child Needs

1. Protein — The "Craving Killer" & Growth Fuel

Most Indian kids eat high carbs but **very low protein.**
When protein is low:

- Kids feel hungry often
- They crave chips, biscuits, chocolates
- Growth slows
- Immunity becomes weak
- Mood becomes unstable

Protein stabilizes blood sugar and **kills junk cravings naturally.**

How to give it (easy Mom Hacks):

- Add a scoop of clean whey protein in milk or smoothies
- Mix protein in dosa batter, roti dough, or pancake mix
- Add to soups and porridges
- Make protein laddoos
- Make protein-rich evening snacks to stop "5 pm hunger attacks"

Your child will feel fuller, calmer, and more focused — and their **height growth improves** because protein is the building block for bones and muscles.

PLANT
PROTEIN

2. Fiber — For Gut Health, Digestion & Happy Moods

Low fiber =
Constipation + bloating + poor appetite + tantrums + cravings + low immunity.

A healthy gut is the foundation of a healthy child.

But most kids barely eat 5–8g fiber (they need 15–25g depending on age).

How Fiber Helps Kids:

- Reduces cravings
- Improves digestion
- Supports immunity
- Makes poop regular (no drama mornings!)
- Stabilizes mood
- Keeps gut microbiome strong

****How to give it:**

- Add chia seeds or psyllium husk in smoothies
- Serve 1 fruit + 1 vegetable daily (not optional)
- Add oats or millets to breakfast
- Add flaxseed powder to chapatis or dosa batter
- Give fiber gummies (kid-approved!)

When the gut is healthy, the child's **brain, mood, and immunity** improve automatically.

3. Calcium + Vitamin D + Magnesium — For Strong Bones & Height

You want your child to reach their **best height potential**, right?

Then understand this:

Height isn't just genetic — it's heavily influenced by nutrition.

Calcium alone doesn't fix it.
Kids need a **combination** of:

- Calcium
- Vitamin D
- Magnesium
- Vitamin K2

This combo supports bone density, posture, sleep, and physical growth.

Mom-approved ways to give it:

- Fortified milk or plant milk
- Chewable calcium-magnesium supplements
- Vitamin D drops (weekly or daily as required)
- Sesame seeds & ragi (natural boosters)

When bones are nourished, height improves and kids sleep better — which further boosts growth.

4. Omega-3 is one of the most *powerful nutrients* for a growing child, and most kids don't get enough of it. It supports:

🧠 Sharper Brain & Focus

Omega-3 (especially DHA) helps build brain cells.
Kids who get enough often show **better focus, memory, and learning ability**.

😌 Better Mood & Emotional Balance

It supports calmness and reduces irritability and mood swings.

👀 Stronger Eyesight

DHA is a major part of the retina. Adequate omega-3 means **better vision**—especially important today because of screen time.

🦴 Height & Bone Support

Omega-3 reduces inflammation, improves nutrient absorption, and supports HGH (growth hormone) activity — indirectly helping **better height growth**.

🦠 Strong Immunity & Gut Health

It helps reduce inflammation in the gut and supports a healthy immune response.

Best Kid-Friendly Sources

- Flaxseeds & chia seeds (powdered for kids)
- Walnuts
- Omega-3 eggs
- Fish (if the family eats non-veg)
- Omega-3 supplements (safe, easy to mix in food)

Common Mom Objections - Answered

"But I want my child to get everything from food."

Of course!
Food is the foundation.

But realistically:

- School tiffin comes back half-eaten
- Kids prefer fast snacks
- Evening hunger spikes
- Nutrient loss in modern farming is real

Supplements don't replace food —
they cover the missing nutrients so your child's body functions at 100%.

"Aren't supplements artificial?"

High-quality supplements are made from pure, concentrated nutrients —
not artificial chemicals.

Think of them as **nutrient insurance**.

Just like we wash vegetables because we want to be safe...
we give supplements so the child's nutrition is safe.

"Will my child become dependent?"

Absolutely not.

Supplements support the body — they don't replace natural functions.
Just like drinking water doesn't create 'dependence,' meeting nutrition needs helps kids:

- Eat better
- Grow better
- Feel better

And eventually, they naturally develop a taste for healthier foods.

"My child won't drink it."

This is where **Smart Mom Hacks** come in:

- Add chocolate/vanilla whey in milk
- Mix in pancakes, rotis, idlis
- Blend into smoothies
- Make energy bars at home
- Add fiber or protein to dosa batter
- Mix in pasta sauce or soups

Once your child's body feels nourished, even their **taste** for food changes.

The Smart-Mom Summary

- Protein kills cravings & supports height
- Fiber heals gut & stabilizes mood
- Calcium/Vit D/Magnesium build strong bones
- Supplements make your life easier
- Healthier kids = happier home

Smart moms don't work harder.
They work smarter.

Supplements are not a shortcut —
they're the **support system** every modern child needs.

🥗 Healthy Food Cheat Sheet for Busy Moms

Quick swaps & smart choices to make kids CRAVE healthy food without fights!

🍎 1. Smart Breakfast Choices

Best options:

- Oats + chia seeds + fruit
- Millet dosa / idli
- Veg omelette
- Almond flour pancakes

- Smoothie with **plant protein**
- Greek yogurt + berries

Avoid: Sugary cereals, bread-butter, chocolate milk.

🍱 2. Lunchbox Heroes (Healthy & Kid-Approved)

Pack more of →

- Paneer / tofu rolls
- Veggie paratha with curd
- Chickpea wraps
- Millet poha/upma
- Rice + dal + ghee + veggies
- Healthy noodles (moringa, millet, quinoa)

Avoid: Maida noodles, chips, biscuits as fillers.

🍿 3. Evening Snack Swaps

Healthy swaps:

- Popcorn (air-popped) instead of chips
- Peanut chaat instead of biscuits
- Fruit smoothies instead of packaged juices
- Roasted makhana instead of wafers
- Cheese toast (multigrain) instead of bakery items

🥦 4. Fiber Boosters (Reduce Junk Cravings!)

Add daily:

- Chia seeds
- Flax seeds
- Fruits (apple, pear, banana)
- Vegetables (broccoli, carrot, cucumber)
- Whole grains (millets, quinoa, oats)
- Good brand Soluble Fiber, can be mixed in water or in any drink. Soluble fiber is food for good bugs in our gut.

Tip:
90% of junk cravings go away when fiber is enough!

💪 5. Protein Essentials (For Height, Strength & Satiety)

Daily sources:

- Paneer
- Lentils/dal
- Tofu
- Eggs
- Greek yogurt
- **Plant protein shake**

Kids need 1g protein per kg body weight per day.

🥛 6. Calcium for Height & Bones

Give more:

- Milk
- Ragi
- Almonds
- Paneer
- Sesame seeds (til)
- Spinach
- Multivitamin + calcium (if needed)

🧠 7. Healthy Fats for Brain & Focus

Use daily:

- Ghee
- Almonds
- Walnuts
- Avocado
- Omega 3 soft gel (EPA + DHA)

These improve **memory, focus, mood & immunity.**

🚫 8. Hidden Junk to Avoid

These look harmless but cause cravings:

- Breads & buns

- Biscuits (even digestive)
- Readymade soups
- Packaged juices
- Flavoured yogurt
- Instant noodles
- Nuggets & fries

💧 9. Hydration Cheat Sheet

Always keep:

- Water bottle
- Lemon water
- Coconut water
- Fruit-infused water

Kids confuse **thirst with hunger** → leads to overeating & junk cravings.

Kids Approved Recipes

1. Healthy Broccoli Soup

Ingredients

- 2 cups broccoli florets
- 1 small onion, chopped
- 2 garlic cloves
- 1 cup coconut milk OR almond milk
- 1 cup vegetable broth
- Salt, pepper
- 1 tsp olive oil
- Optional: 1 tbsp nutritional yeast for cheesy flavor

Method

- Heat oil in a pan, sauté onion + garlic.
- Add broccoli + broth. Cook 10–12 mins until soft.
- Blend until creamy.
- Add coconut/almond milk, salt, pepper.
- Simmer 2 mins and serve.

Healthy Broccoli Soup

2. Almond Flour Wrap

Ingredients

- 1 cup almond flour
- 2 eggs
- 1 tbsp olive oil
- 1/3 cup water
- Salt

Method

- Whisk eggs + water + oil.
- Add almond flour + salt → thin batter.
- Pour a ladle on a non-stick pan like a dosa.
- Cook both sides till lightly golden.
- Fill with veggies / tofu / hummus.

Almond Flour Wrap

3. Tofu Vietnamese Roll

Ingredients

- Rice paper sheets
- 1 cup tofu strips (pan-seared)
- Julienned carrot, cucumber, lettuce
- Fresh mint + coriander
- **Dipping Sauce:** 1 tbsp soy sauce, 1 tsp lime, 1 tsp peanut butter

Method

- Dip rice paper in warm water for 5 seconds.
- Lay on a plate.
- Add tofu, veggies, herbs.
- Roll tightly.
- Serve with dipping sauce.

4. Cheesy Chickpea Quesadilla

Ingredients

- 1 whole wheat tortilla / almond flour wrap
- ½ cup boiled chickpeas (lightly mashed)
- ¼ cup mozzarella or vegan cheese
- 1 tbsp chopped onion + coriander
- Salt, pepper, paprika

Method

- Mash chickpeas with spices.
- Spread on half tortilla.
- Add cheese.
- Fold and toast on both sides till crisp.

Cheesy Chickpea Quesadilla

5. Arrabbiata Pasta

Ingredients

- 1 cup whole wheat / red lentil pasta
- 2 tomatoes (blended)
- 3 garlic cloves
- 1–2 red chillies
- 1 tbsp olive oil
- Salt + oregano + basil

Method

- Boil pasta al dente.
- Heat oil → sauté garlic + chillies.
- Add tomato puree + salt + herbs.
- Cook 10 mins.
- Add pasta → mix well.

Arrabbiata Pasta

6. Moringa Noodles

Ingredients

- 1 pack moringa noodles
- 1 tbsp sesame oil
- 1 cup chopped vegetables
- 1 tsp soy sauce
- 1 tsp lemon juice
- Salt, pepper
- Optional: tofu strips

Method

- Boil noodles, drain.
- Stir-fry vegetables in sesame oil.
- Add noodles + soy sauce.
- Toss well, finish with lemon.

Moringa Noodles

🛒 Kid-Friendly Healthy Grocery List

🥦 VEGETABLES

- Broccoli (2–3 heads)
- Carrots
- Cucumbers
- Cherry tomatoes
- Red, yellow, green bell peppers
- Lettuce / Romaine
- Spinach or mixed greens
- Onions (red + white)
- Garlic
- Raw papaya (if making Som Tom too)
- Moringa noodles veggies: cabbage, beans, spring onion

🌿 HERBS

- Fresh mint
- Fresh coriander
- Fresh basil (optional for Arrabbiata and Thai dishes)

🍊 FRUITS (optional but helpful)

- Lime / lemon (for Vietnamese rolls, noodles, salad)

PANTRY & DRY INGREDIENTS

- Almond flour
- Chickpeas (canned or dry)
- Red lentil or whole wheat pasta
- Jasmine rice (optional)
- Rice paper sheets (for Vietnamese rolls)
- Moringa noodles
- Tortillas (whole wheat or homema
- Olive oil
- Sesame oil
- Soy sauce / Tamari
- Green Thai curry paste (if using for other dishes)
- Tomato purée / fresh tomatoes
- Spices:
- Salt
- Black pepper
- Paprika / chilli flakes
- Oregano
- Italian seasoning
- Garlic powder (optional)

DAIRY / NON-DAIRY

- Coconut milk (for soup or curry)
- Mozzarella or vegan cheese (for chickpea quesadilla)
- Almond milk (for broccoli soup)
- A2 milk

🥚 PROTEIN SOURCES

- Firm tofu
- Eggs (for almond flour wrap)
- Whey or plant protein (optional for smoothies / kids snacks)

🥜 NUTS & SEEDS

- Roasted peanuts (for Vietnamese roll and Som Tom)
- Nutritional yeast (optional for a cheesy flavor in broccoli soup)

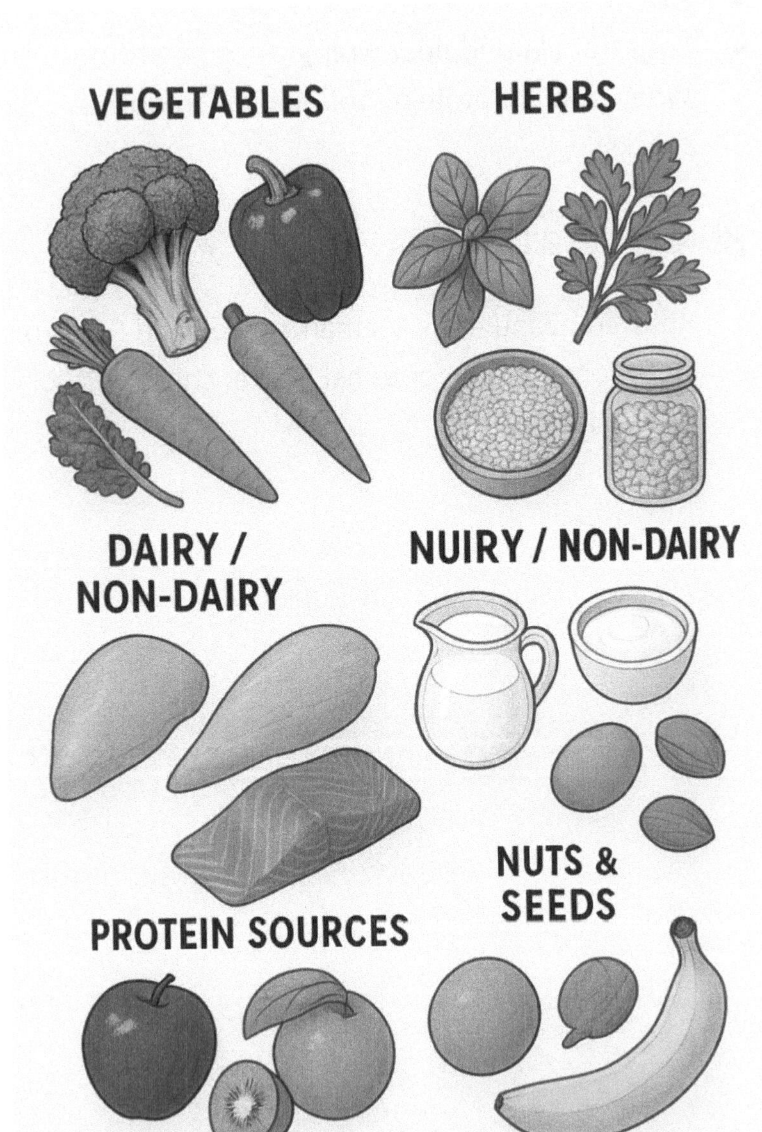
VEGETABLES
HERBS
DAIRY / NON-DAIRY
NUIRY / NON-DAIRY
NUTS & SEEDS
PROTEIN SOURCES

💜 A Note From the Author

"I am a Certified Nutritionist and Metabolic health Coach.
and Above all a mom desperate to help her child eat better.
These hacks changed our home—no more food fights, no more stress.
If they worked for us,
they will work for you too."

About the Author — Meenakshi Rana

Meenakshi Rana is a **Nutritionist** and **Metabolic Health** and **Fertility Coach**, Co-founder of **Fit Family Hit Family**, and a mother who turned her personal struggles into a mission.
For years, she has helped moms build strong routines and raise mindful, healthy eaters through simple, real-life strategies that actually work.

Her warm, relatable approach has made her a trusted guide for thousands of parents across India and beyond.